Bible Colors

An Early Learning Sticker Book • Written by Donna Cooner, Ed.D. • Illustrated by Rusty Fletcher

Broadman & Holman Publishers

God creates the
YELLOW sun
to shine in the sky.

Genesis 1:1-5

Find the sticker of
the yellow sun and
place it in the sky.

Noah bravely builds a big BROWN boat.

Genesis 6

Find the sticker of brown wood and place it near Noah.

God's angel appears in the bright ORANGE flames of a burning bush.

Exodus 3:1-6

Find the stickers of orange flames and place them on the bush.

BLACK locusts blanket
the land of Egypt.

Exodus 10:13-20

Find the stickers of the black locusts and place them on the ground.

The priests play two SILVER trumpets to call the people together.

Numbers 10:1-10

Find the stickers of the silver trumpets and place them in the priests' hands.

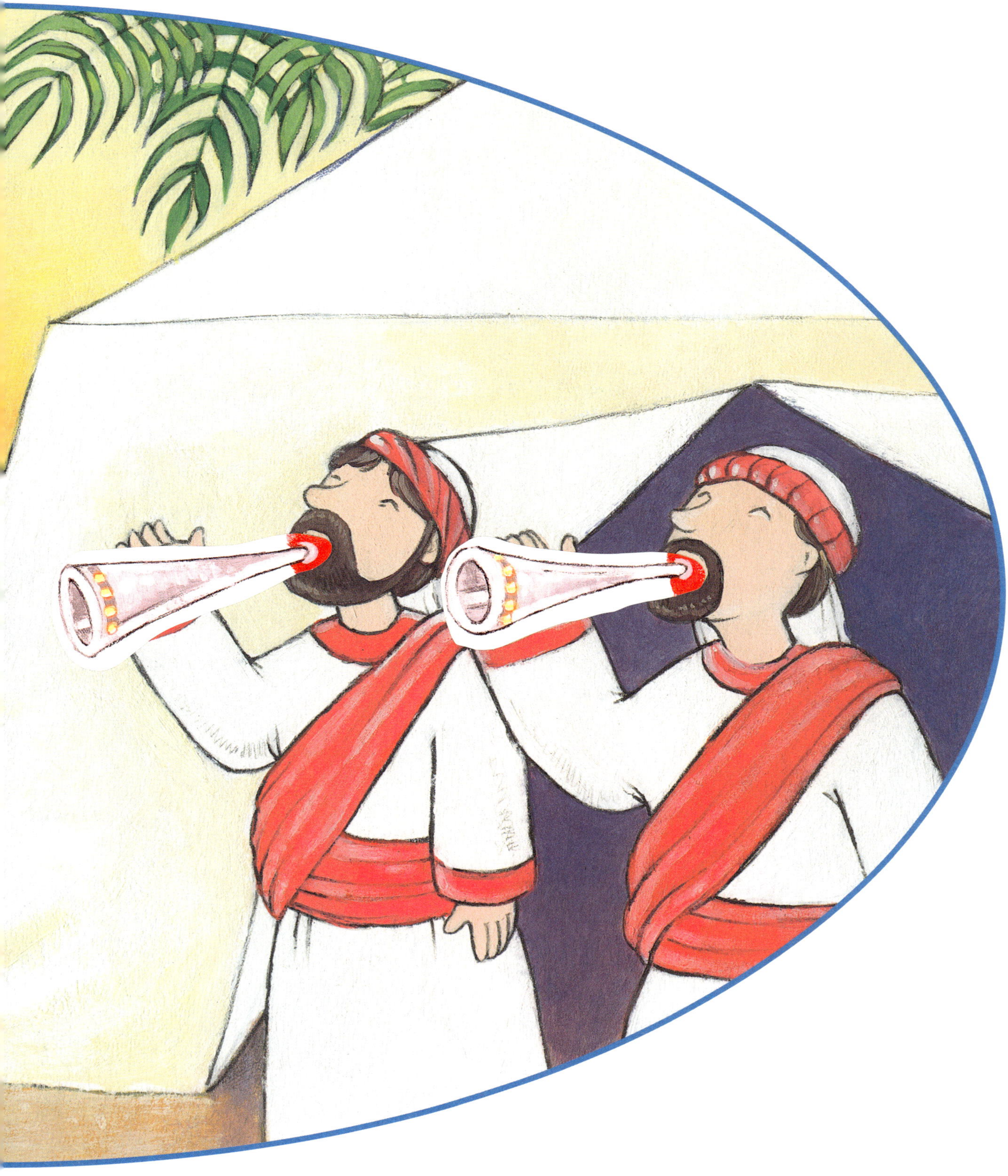

King Solomon built a great temple gleaming with GOLD walls.

1 Kings 6:14-22

Find the sticker of the gold altar and place it in the temple.

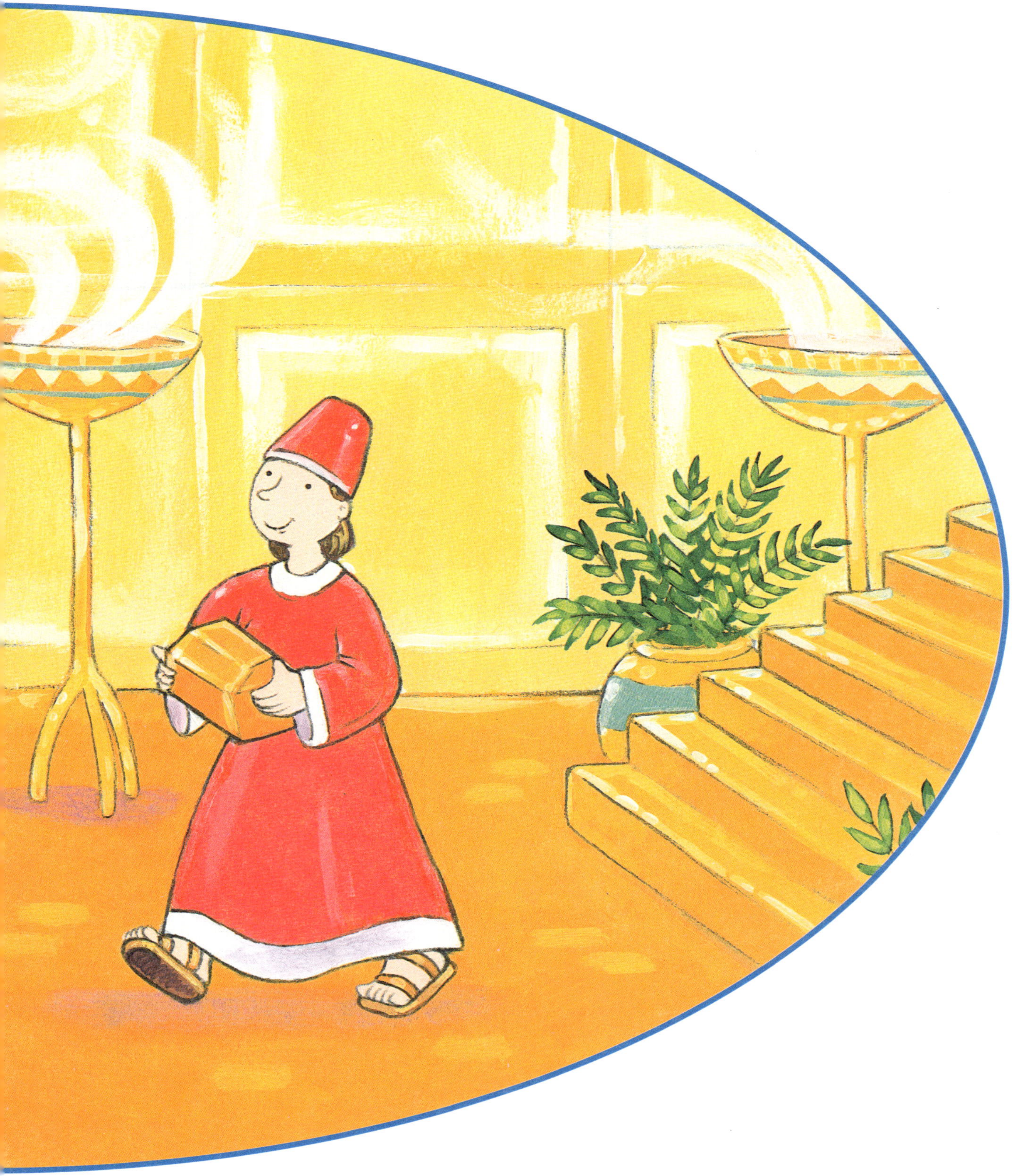

Jesus wears a glowing cloth of WHITE.

Matthew 17:1-2

Find the sticker of white cloth and place it on Jesus.

Jesus greets the group gathered on the GREEN grass.

Mark 6:39-44

Find the sticker of green grass and place it on the hillside.

Jesus turns water into RED wine at a wedding.

John 2:1-11

Find the stickers of red wine and place them on the table.

Simon and his friends throw their fishing nets into the BLUE sea.

John 21:1-6

Find the stickers of the blue waves and place them in the sea.

Lydia sells PURPLE cloth and invites Paul to her house.

Acts 16:14-15

Find the stickers of purple cloth and place them in Lydia's market stall.

Joseph's coat is a
RAINBOW of colors.

Genesis 37:3

Find the sticker of the rainbow-colored coat and place it on Joseph.